I0707889

Thank You
Dear Reader,

We would like to extend our heartfelt gratitude to you for choosing to read [Book Title]. Your support means the world to us, and we hope that this book has enriched your life in some way.

Writing a book is a journey, and it wouldn't have been possible without the encouragement of our friends, family, and the dedicated team that worked tirelessly to bring this project to life. We also want to express our appreciation to our readers, like you, who make all our efforts worthwhile.

As authors, we value your feedback and would love to hear your thoughts on [Book Title]. Please consider leaving a review or reaching out to us on social media or through our website. Your insights will help us continue to improve and create more meaningful content in the future.

Once again, thank you for being a part of this journey with us. We hope that the pages of this book have transported you to new worlds, ignited your imagination, or provided valuable insights.

With sincere appreciation,
Author: Lali Coloring Book

Feel free to customize this "Thank You" page to suit your specific book and personal style. You can add or remove elements as needed to make it more personal and relevant to your readers.